Junior Field Guide

Land Mammals of Nunavut

WRITTEN BY
Jordan Hoffman

ILLUSTRATED BY
Lenny Lishchenko

TABLE OF CONTENTS

WHAT IS A MAMMAL?

Mammals are a large group of many different kinds of animals that share common qualities.

Mammals have hair or fur on their bodies. Some mammals, such as whales, lose this hair shortly after they are born.

Female mammals produce milk to feed their babies. They have structures in their bodies called **mammary glands**, which make milk.

Mammal parents care for their young. Many mammals spend a lot of time and energy caring for their babies to help make sure they live long lives.

Characteristics of mammals

- Mammals have hair or fur.
- Mammals produce milk to feed their babies.
- Mammals care for their young.

There are three groups of mammals: monotremes, marsupials, and placental mammals. Mammals are divided into these groups based on how their young are born. Only placental mammals live in Nunavut.

Monotremes are mammals that lay eggs. The platypus and echidna, or spiny anteater, are the only existing monotremes.

Marsupials are mammals that carry their young in a pouch after birth. Kangaroos and koalas are examples of marsupials.

Placental mammals give birth to well-developed young. Placental mammal babies develop in their mothers longer than other types of mammals. An organ called the placenta provides nutrients to the baby when it is growing inside its mother. Polar bears, walruses, and Arctic foxes are examples of placental mammals.

A platypus is a monotreme.

A kangaroo is a marsupial.

A polar bear is a placental mammal.

5

Adaptations of land mammals in Nunavut

Most mammals live on land and use four limbs to move. Some mammals are adapted to swim, fly, and climb trees. Adaptations are special skills or qualities an animal has that help it survive.

For example, mammals such as seals and whales have flippers for swimming.

Mammals such as bats have wings to fly. Others, such as flying squirrels, have extra skin that stretches between their limbs so they can glide from tree to tree.

Land mammals are adapted to life on land. Land mammals in Nunavut must be adapted for snow, ice, extreme cold temperatures, warm temperatures, predators, times with plenty of food, and times without enough food.

flying squirrel

Land mammals in Nunavut are adapted to their extreme environment in different ways. Some of them **migrate**, some grow thick fur to stay warm all year, some **hibernate**, and others stay beneath the snow to keep warm. Some land mammals in Nunavut learn to run soon after they are born to avoid predators. Others stay in the safety of underground dens until they are ready to survive on their own.

In this field guide, you will find out more about these animals and how they survive the extreme environment in Nunavut.

BROWN LEMMING

Appearance

Brown lemmings are small **rodents**. Male brown lemmings weigh an average of 78 grams, and females weigh an average of 68 grams. Males are about 15 centimetres long, and females are about 14.5 centimetres long.

As their name suggests, brown lemmings have a reddish-brown coat with a grey head and shoulders in the summer. In the winter, they have a longer, greyer coat.

Brown lemmings have a small head with small eyes and ears. Brown lemmings also have feet with long claws for burrowing.

Range

Brown lemmings live all over Nunavut except for the southern part of the Kivalliq region, islands in Hudson Bay, and islands in the High Arctic.

Habitat

Brown lemmings live on the tundra. They are usually found in wetter areas than collared lemmings, such as stream banks, lakeshores, low-lying areas, and rocky areas. They prefer areas covered in grasses, mosses, and **sedges**. These areas help protect their nests and tunnels from the cold in the winter.

Diet

Brown lemmings are **herbivores**. They mainly eat the shoots of grasses. They also eat sedges, moss, bark, twigs, berries, lichens, and the roots of plants.

Reproduction

Brown lemmings usually **breed** from mid-June until early September. In some years they breed all year round, even under the snow.

Young brown lemmings are called pups. Brown lemmings can have between four and nine pups in a **litter**. Sometimes female brown lemmings have a litter every three to four weeks during short breeding seasons.

Behaviour

Brown lemmings do not hibernate. They are active all winter long. Brown lemmings use their claws to dig through snowdrifts in the winter. In the summer, brown lemmings can be active 24 hours a day as they search for food and build tunnels.

COLLARED LEMMING

Appearance

Collared lemmings are small rodents. Male and female collared lemmings weigh between 45 and 115 grams. They are usually between 13 and 16 centimetres long. Collared lemmings are about the same size as brown lemmings, but they have a shorter tail.

Collared lemmings have a summer coat and a winter coat. Their summer coats have grey backs and a black stripe down the middle, a light belly, and brown fur on the chests, shoulders, and legs. Their winter coats are white, and they are longer and thicker than their summer coats.

Collared lemmings have wide, furry feet. They grow large claws on their front feet that they use for burrowing.

Range

Collared lemmings live all over the Qikiqtani region, including the High Arctic islands. They also live in the northeast corner of the Kitikmeot region.

Did you know?

The collared lemming is the only rodent that turns white in the winter.

Habitat

Collared lemmings live on the tundra. They are usually found in drier, rockier areas than brown lemmings. In the winter, they live in low-lying areas with sedges, mosses, and cotton grass. These plants provide good snow cover and insulate the nests and tunnels of collared lemmings.

Diet

Collared lemmings are herbivores. They mainly eat the leaves of dwarf willows and flowering plants. They also eat berries, grasses, sedges, twigs, and the buds of plants.

Reproduction

Collared lemmings breed from early March until early September. In some years, they breed all year round, with only a short break during the spring and summer.

Young collared lemmings are called pups. Females give birth to between one and seven pups at a time. Sometimes female collared lemmings have a litter every three to four weeks during short breeding seasons.

Baby collared lemmings cannot see or hear when they are born. They weigh about 3.8 grams at birth.

Behaviour

Like brown lemmings, collared lemmings do not hibernate. They are active all winter long. Collared lemmings use their claws to dig through snowdrifts to find food and build new tunnels. They also build tunnels in the summer.

Did you know?

Collared lemmings sometimes use dry grasses or *qiviut*—woolly hair from muskoxen—in their nests.

Siksik

Appearance

The siksik, or Arctic ground squirrel, is the largest species of ground squirrel. Adult males weigh around 800 grams, and adult females weigh around 700 grams.

*Siksiit** have a reddish coat in summer and a greyish coat in winter. They have grey, black, and white fur on their backs. They have a long, thin tail with brown and black fur.

siksiit (sik-SEET): plural of siksik, or Arctic ground squirrel

Range

Siksiit live mainly in the Kivalliq and Kitikmeot regions. They are also found in the Qikiqtani region on Melville Peninsula.

Did you know?

Siksiit live farther north than any other squirrel species.

Habitat

Siksiit live on the tundra. They like areas where they can burrow, such as boulder fields and sandy areas.

Diet

Siksiit are **omnivores**. They eat many different kinds of tundra plants, including flowers, berries, and grasses. They also eat eggs, nesting birds, lemmings, and even other siksiit! They also **scavenge** from larger animals.

Reproduction

Siksiit breed in late May after they come out of hibernation. Young siksiit are called pups. Females give birth to between 2 and 10 pups in June.

Pups cannot see or hear when they are born. They do not have teeth or fur. Pups develop quickly and open their eyes when they are about 20 days old. They leave the safety of their family den in late summer. Many pups do not survive their first summer because of predators and harsh weather.

Behaviour

Siksiit live in large groups called colonies. Colonies are made up of an adult male and several females. The adult male controls the area where the colony lives. Adult males sometimes kill young siksiit from other nearby colonies to grow the size of their territory.

Siksiit spend more than half of the year hibernating in underground dens. Their dens can be up to 18 metres long! They enter their dens between September and October and come back out in April or May. Even after they leave their dens in spring, they usually stay close to them while there is still snow on the ground. As the snow melts, siksiit travel along trails formed by their colonies.

Traditional knowledge

The fur of siksiit is soft and can be used for mitts and the inside of parkas.

Did you know?

Male siksiit defend their territory during breeding season and sometimes injure or even kill other males to protect it.

Did you know?

Siksiit are important prey for animals such as wolves, Arctic foxes, grizzly bears, ermines, hawks, and falcons.

Peary Caribou

Appearance

Peary caribou are the smallest type of caribou in North America. Adult females weigh about 60 kilograms, and adult males weigh about 110 kilograms. Females are about 1.4 metres long, and males are about 1.7 metres long.

Peary caribou have a thicker coat than other caribou. In the winter, their coat is long and creamy white. In the spring, their coat becomes shaggy as they lose their winter fur, and it starts to turn brown. In the summer, their coat is brown, with a white belly and white legs.

Peary caribou have short, furry faces, short legs, and wide hooves. Their antlers do not spread out as much as other caribou. They have a grey velvet covering on their antlers.

Range

Peary caribou are found on the High Arctic islands in the Qikiqtani region and Boothia Peninsula in the Kitikmeot region.

Did you know?

Peary caribou are fast. They can often outrun predators such as wolves.

Habitat

Peary caribou live on the tundra.
In summer, they are found in areas with lots of flowering plants, such as the slopes of river valleys and hilltops. In winter, Peary caribou live in areas where there is no snow or ice, or areas with shallow snow, such as higher ground and boulder fields.

Diet

Peary caribou are herbivores. Their favourite plant is purple saxifrage, which they eat in the summer and winter. They also eat grasses, sedges, lichens, willows, and mushrooms.

Did you know?

In June the muzzles of Peary caribou are stained purple because they eat so much purple saxifrage!

Reproduction

Peary caribou breed in the fall. Young Peary caribou are called calves. Females give birth to one calf in the spring. In cold years, calves may not survive because they are not as strong as adults and may have trouble finding food.

Behaviour

Peary caribou do not migrate long distances compared to other species of caribou. They sometimes migrate hundreds of kilometres, but other species of caribou travel thousands of kilometres! Peary caribou can also swim long distances.

Peary caribou need to find food in the winter. When the snow is soft and shallow, they find plants by pushing snow off the ground with their muzzles. Peary caribou use their hooves to dig small clearings when the snow is harder to get through.

Peary caribou are usually found in smaller groups than barren-ground caribou. In summer they are found in groups of 2 to 12 caribou, and in winter in groups of 2 to 4. They are also occasionally found alone.

Traditional knowledge

People from Qausuittuq (Resolute Bay) have said that some Peary caribou will leave areas because of extreme snow and ice covering their food. Peary caribou that do not leave these areas often starve.

15

BARREN-GROUND CARIBOU

Appearance

Barren-ground caribou are medium-sized animals. Adult females weigh about 90 kilograms, and adult males weigh about 150 kilograms.

In the summer, barren-ground caribou have a brown back, chest, and face, with a white belly, white around their hooves, and lighter fur around their necks. In the winter, they have a thick, pale coat with a lighter neck, and a white belly and back end.

Barren-ground caribou have large hooves, a wide muzzle, and short, wide ears. Both male and female barren-ground caribou have antlers. The antlers of barren-ground caribou have a brown velvet covering. Males have larger antlers than females. Males shed their antlers after breeding. Females lose their antlers in late winter or just after their calves are born. Females do not grow antlers every year.

Range

Barren-ground caribou live in the mainland of the Kivalliq and Kitikmeot regions. They also live on Baffin Island, Southampton Island, and islands in northern Hudson Bay.

Habitat

In Nunavut, barren-ground caribou live on the tundra. Barren-ground caribou like to live in places with lots of food and few insects. In winter, they search for areas with soft, shallow snow so they can find food under the snow. Many caribou herds spend the winter in the **boreal forest**. Some herds stay on the tundra during the winter.

Diet

Barren-ground caribou are herbivores. In the summer, they eat plants such as grasses, sedges, shrubs, flowering plants, and mushrooms. In the winter, barren-ground caribou eat lichens, sedges, and dried shrub leaves.

Reproduction

Barren-ground caribou breed in the fall. Young barren-ground caribou are called calves. Females give birth to one calf at a time. Most herds migrate north to have their calves. Females in a herd often have their calves within a few days of each other in the same area.

Did you know?

Calves can run short distances just over an hour after they are born!

Behaviour

Barren-ground caribou are known for their long migrations. Some herds migrate up to 3500 kilometres between their summer and winter habitats. During their migration, they sometimes need to cross rivers. Barren-ground caribou are good swimmers.

Not all barren-ground caribou herds migrate long distances. Some herds migrate as little as 25 kilometres. Barren-ground caribou sometimes travel in groups of hundreds or thousands. They often take a path that avoids predators such as grizzly bears and wolves.

Male barren-ground caribou battle with each other for the ability to breed with females. Males can battle until they are exhausted.

Muskox

Appearance

Muskoxen are large mammals. Male muskoxen can weigh up to 350 kilograms, while females weigh up to 300 kilograms.

Muskoxen have long dark brown or black coats with light hair on their backs and around their feet. Underneath their long coats, they have a dense layer of woolly hair called qiviut. Muskoxen start to look shaggy as they lose their thick winter qiviut in April or May.

Male and female muskoxen have horns that curve down and out into sharp ends. The horns of males are joined at the top of their head, while females have a gap with fur between their horns. Muskoxen also have humped shoulders, short legs, and sharp, rounded hooves.

Range

Muskoxen are found across most of Nunavut except Baffin Island, including the mainland and many High Arctic islands.

Did you know?

Aside from humans, muskoxen have the longest hair of any mammal in North America. Their hair can grow up to 62 centimetres long!

Habitat

Muskoxen live on the tundra. In summer, muskoxen can be found in river valleys, low coastal areas, and open meadows where there are many plants. In winter, muskoxen can be found near hilltops or higher areas where there is not deep snow.

Diet

Muskoxen are herbivores. They eat plants on the tundra such as willows, sedges, and grasses.

Reproduction

Muskoxen breed in late summer. Males have fierce battles. They charge at each other and ram their heads together to determine which males are **dominant**. Dominant males get a chance to breed with females.

Young muskoxen are called calves. Females are pregnant for eight or nine months. They usually give birth to one calf at a time. Calves are born in April or May. Calves can usually stand within an hour of being born. They usually stay close to their mothers for one and a half years.

Behaviour

Muskoxen are usually found in herds of about 15 animals. The size of the herd changes depending on the time of year. Herds are usually led by a dominant male, but sometimes they can be led by a female.

When predators such as wolves threaten muskoxen, the muskoxen often form a circle or semicircle to protect their calves and young. The adults face outward, and calves and young stay in the centre or against one of the adults for protection.

Muskoxen use their sharp hooves to dig through deep and hard-packed snow to find plants in the winter. When the ice is too thick to dig through with their hooves, they use their heavy heads to break through the layers.

Traditional knowledge

The Inuktitut word for muskox is *umingmak*, which means "the bearded one," because of their long hair.

ARCTIC HARE

Appearance

Arctic hares are one of the largest species of hare. Adult males are between 60 and 80 centimetres long, and females are between 60 and 70 centimetres long. Arctic hares weigh between 2.5 and 5.4 kilograms.

Arctic hares are excellent at blending in with their environment. They change colour from white in the winter to brown or grey in the summer. In the most Northern parts of the Arctic, they stay white all year round.

Arctic hares have a white tail, medium-sized ears with black tips, eyes on the sides of their heads, large feet, and long, curved claws.

Range

Arctic hares live all over Nunavut.

Habitat

Arctic hares live on the tundra. In the winter, they often stay in rocky areas and hillsides where the wind blows most of the snow away. In the summer, they are usually found in low, flat areas.

Diet

Arctic hares are omnivores. They eat plants such as grasses, willows, berries, sedges, and sometimes seaweed. Arctic hares sometimes eat meat and have been known to scavenge caribou meat.

Reproduction

Arctic hares breed in April and May. Young Arctic hares are called leverets. Females give birth to between two and eight leverets early in the summer. Females sometimes have two litters in one summer. Leverets are often born in a small hollow in the ground, sometimes near a boulder.

Did you know?

Arctic hare leverets grow twice as fast as other species of hare because of the short summers where they live.

Behaviour

Arctic hares sometimes dig dens or hide behind boulders in blizzards to stay warm. Arctic hares can dig through icy snow with their noses and clawed front paws to reach plants to eat on the tundra below.

Some Arctic hares travel from one place to another depending on the season. In some areas of the Kivalliq region, Arctic hares will leave an area in the summer and come back in November.

Arctic hares can live alone or in family groups. In some areas of the Arctic, they can live in groups of 100 or more!

The number of Arctic hares in an area can go up and down depending on how many predators there are in that area. When there are many predators, such as Arctic wolves, there are usually fewer Arctic hares.

Did you know?

Arctic hares are fast. They can run up to 60 kilometres an hour!

ERMINE

Appearance

Ermines are small weasels. Male ermines are larger than females. Males weigh an average of 80 grams, and females weigh an average of 54 grams. Males are usually up to 35 centimetres long, and females are usually 29 centimetres long. Ermines have very long tails—their tails are almost one-third the length of their entire body.

Ermines have a summer coat and a winter coat. In the summer, they have a brown body, a white belly, and a black tip at the end of the tail. In the winter, ermines turn completely white except for the black tip at the end of their tails.

Ermines have a long body, short legs, a long neck, sharp teeth, short, round ears, and a head shaped like a triangle.

Range

Ermines live all over Nunavut.

Habitat

Ermines live on the tundra. They usually stay close to areas where they can find shelter, such as boulder fields. They are also found near streams and lakes. Sometimes ermines use burrows made by siksiit.

Diet

Ermines are **carnivores**. They mostly eat small mammals, such as siksiit, lemmings, and small Arctic hares. They also sometimes eat bird eggs, birds, and fish.

Reproduction

Ermines breed in late spring or early summer. Young ermines are called kits. Females give birth once a year. They usually give birth to between 4 and 10 kits at a time. Kits are born with their eyes and ears closed and only a thin layer of fur, so their mothers must care for them. Kits reach almost full adult size after only eight weeks.

Behaviour

Ermines need lots of energy to remain active all year, so they eat often. When they have too much food to fill their small stomachs, they store food to eat later. At the beginning of winter, they store many small rodents for future meals.

Ermines are great hunters. They attack by biting the necks of their prey. For larger prey, they bite and hang on until their prey gets too tired to fight back. Ermines can also be aggressive when they are threatened by predators, such as Arctic foxes and snowy owls.

Ermines are active all summer and winter.

WOLVERINE

Appearance

Wolverines are related to weasels. They are the largest member of the weasel family. Wolverines are usually between 80 and 110 centimetres long and between 66 and 86 centimetres tall. Male wolverines are heavier than females. Male wolverines weigh about 15 kilograms, and females weigh about 10.5 kilograms.

Wolverines have a dark brown coat with two lighter stripes along their bodies. They usually have white or orange patches on their chests. Their fur is long and thick to protect them from the cold.

Wolverines have large, furry paws with long, sharp claws. They also have very sharp teeth. Their heads are wide with small black eyes, short, round ears, and a dark snout.

Range

Wolverines live all over Nunavut, except for some of the High Arctic islands.

Did you know?

Wolverines are sometimes called skunk bears, because they look like small bears and leave a strong scent like skunks.

Habitat

In Nunavut, wolverines live on the tundra. They are often found in boulder fields, open areas, and steep areas. They usually stay away from communities and people.

Diet

Wolverines are omnivores. Most of the diet of wolverines is meat. Wolverines feed on smaller prey such as siksiit, Arctic hares, geese, lemmings, and bird eggs. Wolverines can also hunt animals much larger than them, such as caribou. Wolverines are also scavengers. They find meat that is left behind by other predators, such as Arctic foxes, wolves, and grizzly bears. In the summer, wolverines sometimes eat plants and berries.

Reproduction

Wolverines breed in the late spring or summer. Young wolverines are called kits. Kits are usually born in the late winter or early spring. Females usually give birth to two or three kits, but there can be as many as six kits in a litter. Kits are born with a creamy white coat, paws, and face.

Female wolverines build dens in the snow, where they give birth to and raise their young. When kits are still young, they stay in the den, and their mother brings them food. Kits usually stay with their mothers for their first winter and leave to be on their own in the spring. Sometimes kits stay with their mothers for up to two years.

Behaviour

Wolverines are usually found on their own. When wolverines are in groups, it is usually because they are breeding or a mother is with her kits. Wolverines mark their territory and food with a strong scent that keeps other wolverines and animals away.

Wolverines can travel long distances each day to look for food. They sometimes survive for long periods without eating. When there is not much food or when they have too much food, they store meat in cold areas for later.

Wolverines can be very aggressive. Some people say wolverines can even scare off grizzly bears if they are both trying to get the same food!

Traditional knowledge

Inuit in the Kivalliq region say that there are two types of wolverines: one that is larger and lighter coloured, and one that is smaller and darker coloured.

ARCTIC FOX

Appearance

Arctic foxes are related to red foxes, wolves, and dogs. Arctic foxes are the smallest species of the dog family found in Canada. Adult Arctic foxes weigh between 2.5 and 9 kilograms. They are usually between 75 and 115 centimetres long.

Arctic foxes are the only member of the dog family that changes colour in different seasons. Their fur changes from white or pale blue-grey in winter to brown with a light belly and sides in spring and summer. Their coats also change from being long and very thick in the winter to shorter and thinner in the summer.

Arctic foxes have a long and bushy tail, short legs, small, round ears, and a short and rounded muzzle.

Range

Arctic foxes live all over Nunavut.

Did you know?

The Arctic fox has the warmest coat of any animal in the Arctic.

Habitat

Arctic foxes live on the tundra, near the coast, in forested areas, and even out on the sea ice.

Diet

Arctic foxes are carnivores. Lemmings are the largest part of an Arctic fox's diet. They also eat other prey, such as Arctic hare, ptarmigan, bird eggs, siksiit, fish, and the meat of different animals left behind by bears and wolves.

Reproduction

Arctic foxes breed in late winter to early spring. Young Arctic foxes are called pups. Females give birth to an average of 11 pups, but they can have litters of as many as 22 pups! Pups are born between mid-May and mid-June. Pups cannot see or hear when they are born, and they do not have any teeth.

Males bring food to the females while the females take care of the pups. Pups come out of their den when they are between two and four weeks old. Pups are fed by both of their parents until they are ready to take care of themselves. A family of Arctic foxes, including the two parents and an average litter of 11 pups, can eat almost 4000 lemmings before the pups are ready to go out on their own!

Did you know?

The number of Arctic foxes tends to go down when the number of lemmings goes down.

Behaviour

Arctic foxes live in dens that are dug into areas such as the banks of rivers or lakes. They move around from den to den as they search for food. Dens used by Arctic foxes can have nearly 100 entrances and can be over 300 years old! When it is not breeding season or they are not raising young, Arctic foxes usually live alone.

Arctic foxes are good hunters. They can smell and hear small animals living beneath the snow in the winter. Arctic foxes follow animals such as polar bears to eat the meat they leave behind.

Traditional knowledge

Inuit from Mittimatalik (Pond Inlet) say there are two types of Arctic foxes near their community. One type lives on land during the winter, and the other stays on the sea ice. The type that lives on land has thicker and whiter fur and is bigger than the type that lives on the sea ice.

ARCTIC WOLF

Appearance

Arctic wolves are a medium-sized member of the dog family. Adult males weigh between 35 and 40 kilograms, and females weigh between 30 and 35 kilograms. Males are usually between 1.5 and 2 metres long, and females are between 1.4 and 1.8 metres long.

Most Arctic wolves have a white coat. Their coat has two layers. It has long hair to protect them from snow and rain and a very thick, warm undercoat.

Arctic wolves have shorter muzzles, legs, and ears than wolves that live farther south.

Range

Arctic wolves live in the High Arctic islands in the Qikiqtani region.

Habitat

Arctic wolves live on the tundra. They live in different types of habitats depending on where they can find prey.

Diet

Arctic wolves are carnivores. They prefer to eat large mammals such as muskoxen and Peary caribou, but they also eat birds and small mammals such as Arctic hares, lemmings, and Arctic foxes.

Reproduction

Arctic wolves breed once a year in late winter. Young Arctic wolves are called pups. Females usually give birth to litters of five or six pups. Pups are born in dens in late spring or early summer. Pups cannot see or hear when they are born.

Pups stay in the den for the first three weeks of their lives, and they stay close to the den for their first summer. Adult wolves spend a lot of time hunting to feed the pups. Some adults may stay with young pups to care for them.

Behaviour

Arctic wolves live in groups called packs. Wolves in a pack work together to hunt and chase large animals such as muskoxen and caribou. Packs may only get one meal for every 10 animals they chase. Packs often hunt old and young prey in the winter and newborn prey in the summer.

Arctic wolf packs control areas on the tundra called territories. When two Arctic wolf packs are near each other, one pack will often howl at the other to warn that they are in their territory.

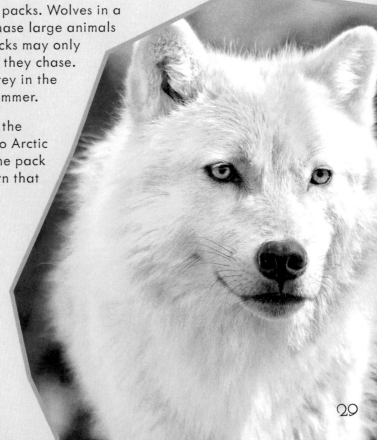

GRIZZLY BEAR

Appearance

Grizzly bears are the second-largest species of bear after polar bears. Adult males can weigh between 250 and 380 kilograms. Adult females weigh about half as much as adult males.

The colour of grizzly bears can range from yellow to brown and black. The bears found on the tundra in Nunavut are often lighter in colour.

Grizzly bears have a hump and long hair on their shoulders. They also have a large head, long snout, and small, round ears. Grizzly bears have long, sharp claws.

Range

Grizzly bears live in the Kivalliq and Kitikmeot regions of Nunavut.

Habitat

Grizzly bears live on the tundra, often in areas with a mix of sand and gravel, areas with taller plants, and areas with lots of lichens. They often live in areas with hills or mountains and along the coast.

Diet

Grizzly bears are omnivores. They eat a variety of foods, including blueberries, crowberries, mountain sorrel, lemmings, birds, siksiit, caribou calves, and ringed seals.

Reproduction

Grizzly bears breed in late spring to early summer. Young grizzly bears are called cubs. Females give birth to between one and four cubs in January or February in a den they have dug in the snow. Most females give birth to two cubs. Cubs are usually about the size of a small squirrel when they are born. Cubs leave the den in the spring and stay with their mothers for up to three years.

Did you know?

Male grizzly bears usually travel much farther than females during the breeding season.

Grizzly bears usually have their first litter when they are five to seven years old. Female grizzly bears usually do not have more than four or five litters in their lifetime.

Behaviour

Grizzly bears are usually found on their own. Sometimes there are groups of grizzly bears feeding in an area with lots of food. Females and younger bears usually stay away from adult males because they sometimes kill cubs and younger bears.

Grizzly bears build dens to stay in for the winter. Grizzly bears are not true **hibernators.** Most animals that hibernate sleep all winter long without waking up, and their body temperature and breathing rate slows down while they hibernate. Grizzly bears sleep most of the winter, but they can be woken up if they are disturbed. Their body temperature and breathing rate only goes down a little bit while they are sleeping.

31

POLAR BEAR

Appearance

Polar bears are the largest species of bear and the largest land carnivore on Earth. Adult males usually weigh between 400 and 600 kilograms, but large males can weigh up to 800 kilograms. Adult females are much less heavy than males, weighing 150 to 250 kilograms. The weight of females can almost double when they are pregnant.

Polar bears' fur varies from bright white to yellow. Unlike most bears, they have a long neck, head, and legs, and small ears.

Polar bears have black noses, sharp teeth, and short but sharp claws.

Range

Polar bears live all over Nunavut.

Did you know?

Polar bears have black skin and semi-transparent fur. This helps them absorb more sunlight to stay warm.

Habitat

Polar bears live on the sea ice during the winter. In the summer, polar bears are found in different habitats, including permanent sea ice and ice floes. In areas where the sea ice melts during the summer, polar bears stay in coastal areas to wait for the ice to freeze again.

Polar bears often prefer to live near sea ice with snowdrifts, open water surrounded by ice, and areas with ice cracks that have refrozen. This is because it is easier for them to find prey in these areas.

Diet

Polar bears are carnivores. They mainly eat ringed seals. They also catch prey such as bearded seals, harp seals, hooded seals, harbour seals, and walruses. Polar bears may also hunt belugas and narwhals when they become trapped in ice. They also sometimes eat bowhead whale carcasses, seabirds, seabird eggs, caribou, and muskoxen.

Reproduction

Polar bears breed in the spring, usually between April and June. Young polar bears are called cubs. Females give birth to one to four cubs between late November and early January in a den they have dug in the snow. Most females give birth to twins. Cubs leave the den in mid-March or early April and stay with their mothers for two and a half years.

Behaviour

Polar bears are expert hunters. Polar bears often wait at the breathing holes of seals. When seals come up for air, polar bears use their sharp claws and teeth to drag them out of the water. In spring, polar bears often hunt for newborn ringed seals under snowdrifts on the sea ice. Polar bears often eat only the fat and skin of ringed seals, depending on how hungry they are.

Polar bears are excellent swimmers. They like to swim between ice floes and across bays. They use their large front paws to swim, just like a dog.

Traditional knowledge

Inuit living in communities on southern Baffin Island have said that the sea ice that polar bears depend on does not freeze as quickly as it used to. They have also said that there is not as much old, thick ice as there once was.

Glossary

boreal forest: a forest that grows in Northern regions with cold temperatures.

breeding: an activity that results in male and female animals producing offspring.

carnivore: an animal that eats other animals as its main food.

dominant: controlling or being more powerful than others.

herbivore: an animal that eats plants as its main food.

hibernate: when animals sleep in a safe place to survive the harshness of winter. While hibernating, animals breathe more slowly, and their body temperature goes down.

hibernators: animals that hibernate during the winter.

litter: a group of young born at one birth.

mammary glands: the milk-producing glands of female mammals.

migrate: move from one place to another according to the seasons.

omnivore: an animal that eats both plants and other animals.

rodent: a mammal with sharp front teeth used for gnawing. Brown lemmings and collared lemmings are examples of rodents.

scavenge: feed on dead animals.

sedges: grass-like plants.